ARTHUR MACHEN

ARTHUR MACHEN

VINCENT STARRETT,
ARTHUR MACHEN

ISBN: 978-93-89956-78-8

Published: 1918

LECTOR HOUSE LLP
E-MAIL: lectorpublishing@gmail.com

ARTHUR MACHEN
A NOVELIST OF ECSTASY AND SIN

BY

VINCENT STARRETT

WITH TWO UNCOLLECTED POEMS BY ARTHUR MACHEN

1918

CONTENTS

Page

NOTE

With singular unanimity critics for thirty years have slighted the work of Arthur Machen. A line suffices for him in Holbrook Jackson's "The Eighteen Nineties," and Mr. Blaikie-Murdoch ignores him completely in "The Renaissance of the Nineties"; yet those are the standard works on the period to which, chronologically, at least, Machen belongs. Mr. Turquet-Milnes, with greater appreciation, gives him a half-chapter in his scholarly work, "The Influence of Baudelaire," but even that is made up largely of quotations from "The Hill of Dreams," to prove Machen a descendent of Baudelaire—an error to which I subscribed until Machen himself disillusioned me, although the assertion is still partially true.

Because, in my opinion, Arthur Machen is the outstanding artist of his time, and one of the great masters of all time, I wrote the following paper, which first appeared in Reedy's *Mirror* for October 5, 1917. That issue is not now obtainable, and, as calls for it continue to come to me and to the publisher, I find ground for a belief that Machen may, at length, be coming into his own, a tardy phenomenon which I am happy to hasten so far as it lies within my power. Mr. Walter M. Hill shares this feeling and this brochure is the result.

I am indebted to Mr. William Marion Reedy for permission to reprint those parts of the article which appeared in his journal.

V.S.

ARTHUR MACHEN

ARTHUR MACHEN

Some thirty odd years ago a young man of twenty-two, the son of a Welsh clergyman, fresh from school and with his head full of a curiously occult medi-aevalism, privately acquired from yellowed palimpsests and dog-eared volumes of black letter, wrote a classic. More, he had it published. Only one review copy was sent out; that was to *Le Livre*, of Paris. It fell into the hands of Octave Uzanne, who instantly ordered Rabelais and Boccaccio to "shove over" on the immortal seats and make room by their side for the author. The book was "The Chronicle of Clemendy"; the author, Arthur Machen.

Three years ago, about, not long after the great war first shook the world, a London evening newspaper published inconspicuously a purely fictional account of a supposed incident of the British retreat from Mons. It described the miraculous intervention of the English archers of Agincourt at a time when the British were sore pressed by the German hordes. Immediately, churchmen, spiritualists, and a host of others, seized upon it as an authentic record and the miracle as an omen. In the hysteria that followed, Arthur Machen, its author, found himself a talked-of man, because he wrote to the papers denying that the narrative was factual. Later, when his little volume, "The Bowmen and Other Legends of the War," appeared in print, it met with an extraordinary and rather impertinent success.

But what had Machen been doing all those long years between 1885 and 1914?

In a day of haphazard fiction and rodomontade criticism, the advent of a master workman is likely to be unheralded, if, indeed, he is fortunate enough to find a publisher to put him between covers. Mr. Machen is not a newcomer, however, as we have seen; no immediate success with a "best seller" furnishes an incentive for a complimentary notice. He is an unknown, in spite of "Clemendy," in spite of "The Bowmen," in spite of everything. For thirty years he has been writing English prose, a period ample for the making of a dozen reputations of the ordinary kind, and in that time he has produced just ten books. In thirty years Harold Bindloss and Rex Beach will have written one-hundred-and-ten books and sold the moving picture rights of them all.

Of course, it is exactly because he does not write books of the ordinary kind that Arthur Machen's reputation as a writer was not made long ago. His apotheosis will begin after his death. The insectial fame of the "popular" novelist is immediate; it is born at dawn and dies at sunset. The enduring fame of the artist too often is born at sunset, but it is immortal.

More than Hawthorne or Tolstoy, Machen is a novelist of the soul. He writes of a strange borderland, lying somewhere between Dreams and Death, peopled with shades, beings, spirits, ghosts, men, women, souls—what shall we call them?—the very notion of whom stops vaguely just short of thought. He writes of the life Satyr-ic. For him Pan is not dead; his votaries still whirl through woodland windings to the mad pipe that was Syrinx, and carouse fiercely in enchanted forest grottoes (hidden somewhere, perhaps, in the fourth dimension!). His meddling with the crucibles of science is appalling in its daring, its magnificence, and its horror. Even the greater works of fictional psychology—"Dr. Jekyll and Mr. Hyde," if you like—shrink before his astounding inferences and suggestions.

It is his theory that the fearful and shocking rites of the Bacchic cultus survive in this disillusioned age; that Panic lechery and wickedness did not cease with the Agony, as Mrs. Browning and others would have us believe.

Of Hawthorne, Arthur Symons wrote: "He is haunted by what is obscure, dangerous, and on the confines of good and evil." Machen crosses those perilous frontiers. He all but lifts the veil; himself, indeed, passes beyond it. But the curtain drops behind him and we, hesitating to follow, see only dimly the phantasmagoria beyond; the ecstasies of vague shapes with a shining about them, on the one hand; on the other the writhings of animate gargoyles. And we experience, I think, a distinct sense of gratitude toward this terrible guide for that we are permitted no closer view of the mysteries that seem to him so clear.

We glimpse his secrets in transfiguring flashes from afar, as Launcelot viewed the San Graal, and, like that tarnished knight, we quest vainly a tangible solution, half in apprehension, always in glamour. But it is like Galahad we must seek the eternal mysteries that obsess Arthur Machen. There is no solution but in absolution, for it is the mysteries of life and death of which he writes, and of life-in-death and death-in-life. This with particular reference to Machen's two most important books, "The House of Souls" and "The Hill of Dreams," in which he reaches his greatest stature as a novelist of the soul.

There are those who will call him a novelist of Sin, quibbling about a definition. With these I have no quarrel; the characterizations are synonymous. His books exhale all evil and all corruption; yet they are as pure as the fabled waters of that crystal spring De Leon sought. They are pervaded by an ever-present, intoxicating sense of sin, ravishingly beautiful, furiously Pagan, frantically lovely; but Machen is a finer and truer mystic than the two-penny occultists who guide modern spiritualistic thought. If we are to subscribe to his curious philosophy, to be discussed later, we must believe that there is no paradox in this.

But something of what we are getting at is explained in his own pages, in this opening paragraph from his story, "The White People," in "The House of Souls": "'Sorcery and sanctity,' said Ambrose, 'these are the only realities. Each is an ecstasy, a withdrawal from the common life.'" And, a little later, in this: "'There is something profoundly unnatural about sin ... the essence of which really is in the taking of heaven by storm.'"

One gathers from a general vagueness on the subject that sin is not popular in these times. There are, of course, new sins and advanced sins and higher sins, all of which are intensely interesting. The chief puzzle to the lay mind is why they should bear these names, since they are usually neither new, advanced and high, nor particularly sinful. I am speaking of sin as an offense against the nature of things, and of evil in the soul, which has very little to do with the sins of the statute book. Sin, according to the same Ambrose I have quoted, is conceivable in the talking of animals. If a chair should walk across a room, that would be sinful, or if a tree sat down with us to afternoon tea. The savage who worships a conjurer is a far finer moralist than the civilise who suspects him—and I use the name moralist for one who has an appreciation of sin.

This is not the sin of the legal code. *Ambrose* I conceive to be Arthur Machen. There are only two realities; sorcery and sanctity—sin and sainthood—and each is an ecstasy. Arthur Machen's is the former.

Perhaps his most remarkable story—certainly I think his most terrible story, is "The Great God Pan," at first published separately with "The Inmost Light"; now occurring in "The House of Souls." It is the story of an experiment upon a girl, as a result of which, for a moment, she is permitted a sight of the Great God, beyond the veil, with shocking consequences. Yet it is told with exquisite reticence and grace, and with a plausibility that is as extraordinary as it is immoral. Here is the conclusion of that story:

> "What I said Mary would see, she saw, but I forgot that no human eyes could look on such a vision with impunity. And I forgot, as I have just said, that when the house of life is thus thrown open, there may enter in that for which we have no name, and human flesh may become the veil of a horror one dare not express.... The blackened face, the hideous form upon the bed, changing and melting before your eyes from woman to man, from man to beast, and from beast to worse than beast, all the strange horror that you witnessed, surprises me but little. What you say the doctor you sent for saw and shuddered at, I noticed long ago; I knew what I had done the moment the child was born, and when it was five years old I surprised it, not once or twice, but several times, with a playmate, you may guess of what kind.... And now Helen is with her companions."

There is the very quintessence of horror in the unutterable suggestion of such passages. As for "The Hill of Dreams," I have found its reading one of the most desolate and appalling experiences in literature. Reading it, himself, years after publication, its author decided that it was a "depressing book." That is undoubtedly true, but spiritually as well as technically it marks to date the topmost pinnacle of his tormented genius. It reaches heights so rarefied that breathing literally becomes painful. To the casual reader this sounds absurd; hyperbolical if not hypocritical rant; but in a day when a majority of critics find it difficult to restrain themselves in speaking of Harold Bell Wright, and place Jeffery Farnol beside Fielding and Thackeray, one cannot go far wrong in indulging a few enthusiasms for so genuine an artist as Arthur Machen.

Of the reviewers into whose hands fell this remarkable book, in the year of its publication, 1907, only one appears to have valued it at its real worth—the editor of *The Academy*, who, carried away by the tale and its telling, turned out a bit of critical prose which might have been lifted from the book, itself. "There is something sinister in the beauty of Mr. Machen's book," he wrote. "It is like some strangely shaped orchid, the colour of which is fierce and terrible, and its perfume is haunting to suffocation by reason of its intolerable sweetness. The cruelty of the book is more savage than any of the cruelty which the book describes. Lucian shuddered at the boys who were deliberately hanging an ungainly puppy; he had thrashed the little ruffian who kicked the sick cat, before he wrapped himself away from the contact of such infamy in the shelter of his own imaginings. For in 'The Hill of Dreams' you seem to be shown a lovely, sensitive boy who has fashioned himself a white palace of beauty in his own mind. He has had time only to realize its full beauty when disease lays its cold touch upon him, and gathers him into her grasp, until he lies decaying and horrible, seeing his own decay and seeing that his decay makes the white palace foul. The boys did not chant songs as they looped the string round the neck of the uncouth puppy. Mr. Machen fashions prose out of the writhings of Lucian, who is dear to him: and his prose has the rhythmic beat of some dreadful Oriental instrument, insistent, monotonous, haunting; and still the soft tone of one careful flute sounds on, and keeps the nerves alive to the slow and growing pain of the rhythmic beat. Lucian in ecstacy of worship for the young girl whose lips have given him a new life, pressed his body against sharp thorns until the white flesh of his body was red with drops of blood. That, too, is the spirit of the book. It is like some dreadful liturgy of self-inflicted pain, set to measured music: and the cadence of that music becomes intolerable by its suave phrasing and perfect modulation. The last long chapter with its recurring themes is a masterpiece of prose, and in its way unique."

After that, there would seem to be no need for further comment on "The Hill of Dreams." But there is—there is!

Quite as important as what Mr. Machen says is his manner of saying it. He possesses an English prose style which in its mystical suggestion and beauty is unlike any other I have encountered. There is ecstacy in his pages. Joris-Karl Huysmans in a really good translation suggests Machen better, perhaps, than another; both are debtors to Baudelaire.[1]

The "ecstasy" one finds in Machen's work (of which more anon) is due in no small degree to his beautiful English "style"—an abominable word. But Machen is no mere word-juggler. His vocabulary, while astonishing and extensive, is not affectedly so. Yet his sentences move to sonorous, half-submerged rhythms, swooning with pagan color and redolent of sacerdotal incense. What is the secret of this graceful English method? It is this: he achieves his striking results and effects through his noteworthy gift of selection and arrangement. I had reached this conclusion, I think, before I encountered a passage from "The Hill of Dreams,"

---

[1] I have let this last assertion stand as part of the original article, although Mr. Machen writes me that I am in error. "I never read a line of Baudelaire," he says, "but I have read deeply in Poe, who, I believe, derives largely from Baudelaire." Of course, it is the other way 'round, Baudelaire derives from Poe, but my own assumption is rendered clear.—V.S.

which clinched it:

> "Language, he understood, was chiefly important for the beauty of its sounds, by its possession of words resonant, glorious to the ear, by its capacity, when exquisitely arranged, of suggesting wonderful and indefinable impressions, perhaps more ravishing and further removed from the domain of strict thought than the impressions excited by music itself. Here lay hidden the secret of suggestion, the art of causing sensation by the use of words."

Was it ever better expressed? He defines his method and exhibits its results at the same time. And dipping almost at random into the same volume, here is a further example of the method:

> "Slowly and timidly he began to untie his boots, fumbling with the laces, and glancing all the while on every side at the ugly, misshapen trees that hedged the lawn. Not a branch was straight, not one was free, but all were interlaced and grew one about another; and just above ground, where the cankered stems joined the protuberant roots, there were forms that imitated the human shape, and faces and twining limbs that amazed him. Green mosses were hair, and tresses were stark in grey lichen; a twisted root swelled into a limb; in the hollows of the rooted bark he saw the masks of men.... As he gazed across the turf and into the thicket, the sunshine seemed really to become green, and the contrast between the bright glow poured on the lawn and the black shadows of the brake made an odd flickering light in which all the grotesque postures of stem and root began to stir; the wood was alive. The turf beneath him heaved and sunk as with the deep swell of the sea...."

And:

> "He could imagine a man who was able to live on one sense while he pleased; to whom, for example, every impression of touch, taste, hearing, or seeing should be translated into odor; who at the desired kiss should be ravished with the scent of dark violets, to whom music should be the perfume of a rose garden at dawn."

This is not prose at all, but poetry, and poetry of a high order. And it is from such beautiful manipulation of words, phrases, and rhythms that Machen attains his most clairvoyant and arresting effects in the realms of horror, dread, and terror; from the strange gesturings of trees, the glow of furnace-like clouds, the somber beauty of brooding fields, and valleys all too still, the mystery of lovely women, and all the terror of life and nature seen with the understanding eye.

So much for Arthur Machen as a novelist. It is a fascinating subject, but it is also an extensive one, and the curious, tenuous quality of his work may lead one into indiscretions

The peculiar philosophy of Arthur Machen is set down in "Hieroglyphics" and in "Dr. Stiggins: His Views and Principles." The first chapter of the latter work is a scathing satire on certain foibles and idiosyncracies of the American people—such as lynching, vote-buying, and food-adulteration—but as it is, on the whole, a polemical volume which, by the nature of the subjects it treats, can have less permanent interest than the author's other work, it may be put to one side; although as a specimen of Machen's impeccable prose it must not be ignored.

In "Hieroglyphics" he returns to those ecstasies mentioned in "The White People" and gives us further definitions. The word ecstasy is merely a symbol; it has many synonyms. It means rapture, adoration, a withdrawal from common life, the other things. "Who can furnish a precise definition of the indefinable? They (the 'other things') are sometimes in the song of a bird, sometimes in the whirl of a London street, sometimes hidden under a great, lonely hill. Some of us seek them with most hope and the fullest assurance in the sacring of the mass, others receive tidings through the sound of music, in the color of a picture, in the shining form of a statue, in the meditation of eternal truth."

"Hieroglyphics" is Arthur Machen's theory of literature, brilliantly exposited by that "cyclical mode of discoursing" that was affected by Coleridge. In it he promulgates the admirable doctrine that fine literature must be, in effect, an allegory and not the careful history of particular persons. He seeks a mark of division which is to separate fine literature from mere literature, and finds the solution in the one word ecstasy (or, if you prefer, beauty, wonder, awe, mystery, sense of the unknown, desire for the unknown), with this conclusion: "If ecstasy be present, then I say there is fine literature, if it be absent, then, in spite of all the cleverness, all the talents, all the workmanship and observation and dexterity you may show me, then, I think, we have a product (possibly a very interesting one) which is not fine literature."

Following this reasoning, by an astonishing sequence of arguments, he proceeds to the bold experiment of proving "Pickwick" possessed of ecstasy, and "Vanity Fair" lacking it. The case is an extreme one, he admits, deliberately chosen to expound his theory to the nth. degree. The analytical key to the test is found in the differentiation between art and artifice, a nice problem in such extreme instances as Poe's "Dupin" stories and Stevenson's "Dr. Jekyll and Mr. Hyde," as Mr. Machen points out. By this ingenious method the "Odyssey," "Oedipus," "Morte D'Arthur," "Kubla Khan," "Don Quixote," and "Rabelais" immediately are proven fine literature; a host of other esteemed works merely, if you like, good literature.

"Pantagruel" by a more delicate application of the test becomes a finer work than "Don Quixote," and in the exposition of this dictum we come upon one of the mountain peaks of Machen's amazing philosophy.

He begins the discussion with a jest about the enormous capacity for strong drink exhibited by *Mr. Pickwick* and his friends, and reminds us that it was the god of wine in whose honor Sophocles wrote his dramas and choral songs, who was worshipped and invoked at the Dionysiaca; and that all the drama arose from the celebration of the Bacchic mysteries. He goes on to the "Gargantua" and "Pantagruel," which reek of wine as Dickens does of brandy and water.

The Rabelaisian history begins: *"Grandgousier estoit bon raillard en son temps, aimant à boire net,"* and ends with the Oracle of the Holy Bottle, with the word *"Trinch ... un mot panomphée, celebré et entendu de toutes nations, et nous signifie, beuvez."* "And I refer you," continues Machen, "to the allocution of Bacbuc, the priestess of the Bottle, at large. 'By wine,' she says, 'is man made divine,' and I may say that if you have not got the key to these Rabelaisian riddles, much of the value—the highest value—of the book is lost to you."

Seeking the meaning of this Bacchic cultus, this apparent glorification of drunkenness in all lands and in all times, from Ancient Greece through Renascent France to Victorian England, by peoples and persons not themselves given to excess, he finds it again in the word ecstasy.

> "We are to conclude that both the ancient people and the modern writers recognized ecstasy as the supreme gift and state of man, and that they chose the Vine and the juice of the Vine, as the most beautiful and significant symbol of that Power which withdraws a man from the common life and the common consciousness, and taking him from the dust of earth, sets him in high places, in the eternal world of ideas ... Let us never forget that the essence of the book ('Pantagruel') is in its splendid celebration of ecstasy, under the figure of the Vine."

At this point Mr. Machen places the "key" in our hands and declines further to reveal his secrets. In *Mr. Pickwick's* overdose of milk punch we are to find, ultimately, "a clue to the labyrinth of mystic theology."

By his own test we are enabled to place Arthur Machen's greatest works on the shelf with "Don Quixote" and "Pantagruel"; by his own test we find the ecstasy of which he speaks in his own pages, under the symbol of the Vine, and under figures even more beautiful and terrible. For minor consideration he finds in Rabelais another symbolism of ecstasy:

> "The shape of gauloiserie, of gross, exuberant gaiety, expressing itself by outrageous tales, outrageous words, by a very cataract of obscenity, if you please, if only you will notice how the obscenity of Rabelais transcends the obscenity of common life; his grossness is poured out in a sort of mad torrent, in a frenzy, a very passion of the unspeakable."

In Cervantes he finds the greater deftness, the finer artifice, but he believes the conception of Rabelais the higher because it is the more remote. *Pantagruel's* "more than frankness, its ebullition of grossness ... is either the merest lunacy, or else it is sublime." And the paragraph that succeeds this one in the book, perhaps it is part of the same paragraph, sums up this astonishing philosophy with a conclusion calculated to shock the Puritanic. Thus:

> "Don't you perceive that when a certain depth has been

passed you begin to ascend into the heights? The Persian poet expresses the most transcendental secrets of the Divine Love by the grossest phrases of the carnal love; so Rabelais soars above the common life, above the streets and the gutter, by going far lower than the streets and the gutter: he brings before you the highest by positing that which is lower than the lowest, and if you have the prepared, initiated mind, a Rabelaisian 'list' is the best preface to the angelic song. (!) All this may strike you as extreme paradox, but it has the disadvantage of being true, and perhaps you may assure yourself of its truth by recollecting the converse proposition—that it is when one is absorbed in the highest emotions that the most degrading images will intrude themselves."

And so on.... The sense of the futility almost of attempting to explain Machen becomes more pronounced as I progress. You will have to read him. You will find his books (if you are fortunate) in a murky corner of some obscure second-hand bookshop.

Arthur Machen was born in Wales in 1863. He is married and has two children. That is an astonishing thought, after reading "The Inmost Light." It is surprising indeed to learn that he was *born*. He is High Church, "with no particular respect for the Archbishop of Canterbury," and necessarily subconsciously Catholic, as must be all those "lonely, awful souls" who write ecstasy across the world. He hates puritanism with a sturdier hatred than inspires Chesterton; for a brilliant exposition of this aversion I commend readers to his mocking introduction to "The House of Souls." That work, "The Hill of Dreams," and "Hieroglyphics" were written between 1890 and 1900, after which their author turned strolling player and alternated for a time between the smartest theatres in London and the shabbiest music halls in London's East End. For the last six years or so he has been a descriptive writer on the London *Evening News*.

His works not before mentioned comprise a translation (the best) of the "Heptameron"; "Fantastic Tales," a collection of mediaeval whimsies, partly translated and partly original and altogether Rabelaisian and delightful; "The Terror," a "shilling shocker" (his own characterization), but a finer work withal than most of the "literature" of the day, and "The Great Return," an extraordinary short tale which may find place some day in another such collection as "The House of Souls."

I have mentioned "The Chronicle of Clemendy," calling it a classic, and something further should be said about that astonishing book. It is the Welsh "Heptameron," a chronicle of amorous intrigue, joyous drunkenness, and knightly endeavor second to none in the brief muster of the world's greatest classics. In it there is the veritable flavour of mediaeval record. Somewhat less outspoken than Balzac in his "Droll Stories," and less verbose than Boccaccio, Machen proves himself the peer of either in gay, irresponsible, diverting, unflagging invention, while his diction is lovelier than that of any of his forerunners, including the nameless authors of those rich Arabian tapestries which were the parent tales of all mediaeval and modern facetiae.

The day is coming when a number of serious charges will be laid against us who live in this generation, and some severe questions asked, and the fact that we will be dead, most of us, when the future fires its broadside, has nothing at all to do with the case.

We are going to be asked, *post-mortem*, why we allowed Ambrose Bierce to vanish from our midst, unnoticed and unsought, after ignoring him shamefully throughout his career; why Stephen Crane, after a few flamboyant reviews, was so quickly forgotten at death; why Richard Middleton was permitted to swallow his poison at Brussels; why W.C. Morrow and Walter Blackburn Harte were in our day known only to the initiated, discriminating few; their fine, golden books merely rare "items" for the collector. Among other things, posterity is going to demand of us why, when the opportunity was ours, we did not open our hearts to Arthur Machen and name him among the very great.

TWO UNCOLLECTED POEMS

THE REMEMBRANCE OF THE BARD

In the darkness of old age let not my memory fail:
Let me not forget to celebrate the beloved land of Gwent.
If they imprison me in a deep place, in a house of pestilence,
Still shall I be free, remembering the sunshine upon Mynydd
Maen.
There have I listened to the song of the lark, my soul has ascend-
ed with the song of the little bird:
The great white clouds were the ships of my spirit, sailing to the
haven of the Almighty.
Equally to be held in honour is the site of the Great Mountain.
Adorned with the gushing of many waters— sweet is the shade
of its hazel thickets.
There a treasure is preserved which I will not celebrate;
It is glorious and deeply concealed.
If Teils should return, if happiness were restored to the Cymri,
Dewi and Dyfrig should serve his Mass; then a great marvel
would be made visible.
O blessed and miraculous work! then should my bliss be as the
joy of angels.
I had rather behold this offering than kiss the twin lips of dark
Gwenllian.
Dear my land of Gwent: *O quam dilecta tabernacula*. Thy rivers
are like precious golden streams of Paradise, thy hills are as the
Mount Syon.
Better a grave on Twyn Barlwm than a throne in the palace of the
Saxons at Caer-Ludd.

ARTHUR MACHEN

THE PRAISE OF MYFANWY

O gift of the everlasting:
O wonderful and hidden mystery.
Many secrets have been vouchsafed to me,
I have been long acquainted with the wisdom of the trees;
Ash and oak and elm have communicated to me from my boy-
hood,
The birch and the hazel and all the trees of the greenwood have
not been dumb.
There is a caldron rimmed with pearls of whose gifts I am not
ignorant;
I will speak little of it; its treasures are known to the Bards.
Many went on the search of Caer-Pedryfan,
Seven alone returned with Arthur, but my spirit was present.
Seven are the apple-trees in a beautiful orchard;
I have eaten of their fruit which is not bestowed on Saxons.
I am not ignorant of a Head which is glorious and venerable;
It made perpetual entertainment for the warriors, their joys
would have been immortal;
If they had not opened the door of the south, they would have
feasted for ever,
Listening to the song of the fairy Birds of Rhiannon.
Let not anyone instruct me concerning the Glassy Isle;
In the garments of the saints who returned from it were rich
odours of Paradise.
All this I knew, and yet my knowledge was ignorance.
For one day, as I walked by Caer-rhiu in the principal forest of
Gwent,
I saw golden Myfanwy as she bathed in the brook Tarogi,
Her hair flowed about her; Arthur's crown had dissolved into a
shining mist.
I gazed into her blue eyes as it were into twin heavens,
All the parts of her body were adornments and miracles.
O gift of the everlasting:
O wonderful and hidden mystery:
When I embraced Myfanwy a moment became immortality.

ARTHUR MACHEN

Lector House believes that a society develops through a two-fold approach of continuous learning and adaptation, which is derived from the study of classic literary works spread across the historic timeline of literature records. Therefore, we aim at reviving, repairing and redeveloping all those inaccessible or damaged but historically as well as culturally important literature across subjects so that the future generations may have an opportunity to study and learn from past works to embark upon a journey of creating a better future.

This book is a result of an effort made by Lector House towards making a contribution to the preservation and repair of original ancient works which might hold historical significance to the approach of continuous learning across subjects.

HAPPY READING & LEARNING!

LECTOR HOUSE LLP
E-MAIL: lectorpublishing@gmail.com